I CAN Live For Jesus!

A Companion Book to "Heaven How To Live Til We Get There"

Written by Lynnette Maynor
Illustrated by Judy Plumley
Post Illustration, Design, and Formatting by Starry Eyes Media, Princeton, WV
www.StarryEyes.Media

All rights reserved solely by the author. The author guarantees all contents are original and do not infringe upon the legal rights of any other person or work. **Individual and group copies and use permitted. Not for resale.**

Scripture quotations taken from the King James Version (KJV) – public domain.

Copyright © 2018 Lynnette Maynor
www.LynnetteMaynor.com

...For Him...

**The Kingdom of Heaven is perfect!
It has sparkling jewels and a street of gold!**

God's throne is in Heaven. He rules with love and kindness.

Heaven is a beautiful place of light and life!

Heaven is a place of peace.

**There is joy in Heaven!
There are no tears or sadness there.**

**There is no darkness or night in Heaven.
The glory of God is the light!**

We can go to Heaven one day when we say "Yes!"
and receive Jesus into our lives.
That's when our sins are taken away
and we become God's children.

**Once we receive Jesus we have invisible armor to wear.
It protects us from Satan, our enemy, until we go to Heaven.**

God gives His children a shield of faith to stop Satan's lies. Faith is believing the truths of God when Satan tries to lie to us.

**Reading the Bible is important. It is God's book of truths.
It helps our faith to grow.**

Church is a caring place to go to honor God and be with others who love Him. It's a special place to learn more about God and His great love.

**Praise and worship bring great glory to God!
It gives Him the highest honor and says that He is The Lord!**

Jesus is the perfect Son of God. He wants us to believe in Him and receive Him as our Savior.

Jesus died on the cross for the whole world because He loves everyone. He did this so our sins could be washed away with His blood and we could become His forever friends.

Jesus was buried in a tomb.

Jesus came back to life in only three days! He said, "Because I live you shall live also." How wonderful to live with Him forever!

You can receive Jesus as your Savior.
Here is what you can say to God...

Dear God,
I know I have sinned, done wrong things, and I am sorry. I believe Jesus died on the cross for my sins and came back to life. I open my heart and invite Jesus into my life now. Thank You for forgiving me and washing away all my sins with the blood of Jesus.

Thank You for hearing my prayer and coming into my life. Thank You for loving me! I Love You too!

I can receive Jesus now!

Once you receive Jesus it will seem He's right beside you. His Holy Spirit will guide, protect, and comfort you. He will give you loving care and help you live for Him.

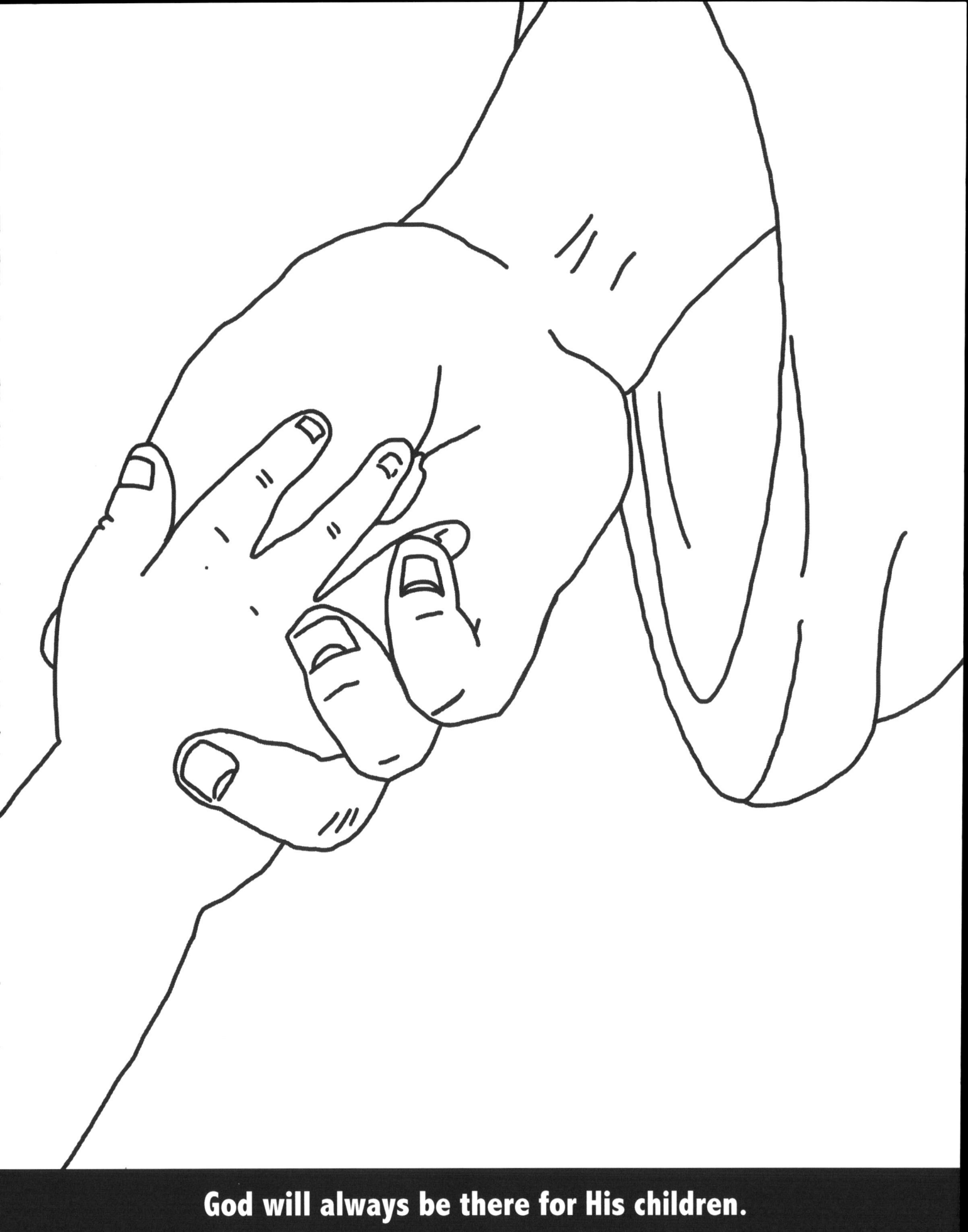

**God will always be there for His children.
The Bible says He holds us by the hand.**

God places beautiful things in His children's lives called fruits of His Holy Spirit. They are love, joy, peace, patience, kindness, goodness, faithfulness, gentleness and self control. They are so sweet, helping us live the lives He has planned for us!

God want us to tell others about Jesus so they can accept Him into their lives.

**We can shine our lights of love
so others can see the way to Jesus.**

We can show people the way to Jesus.

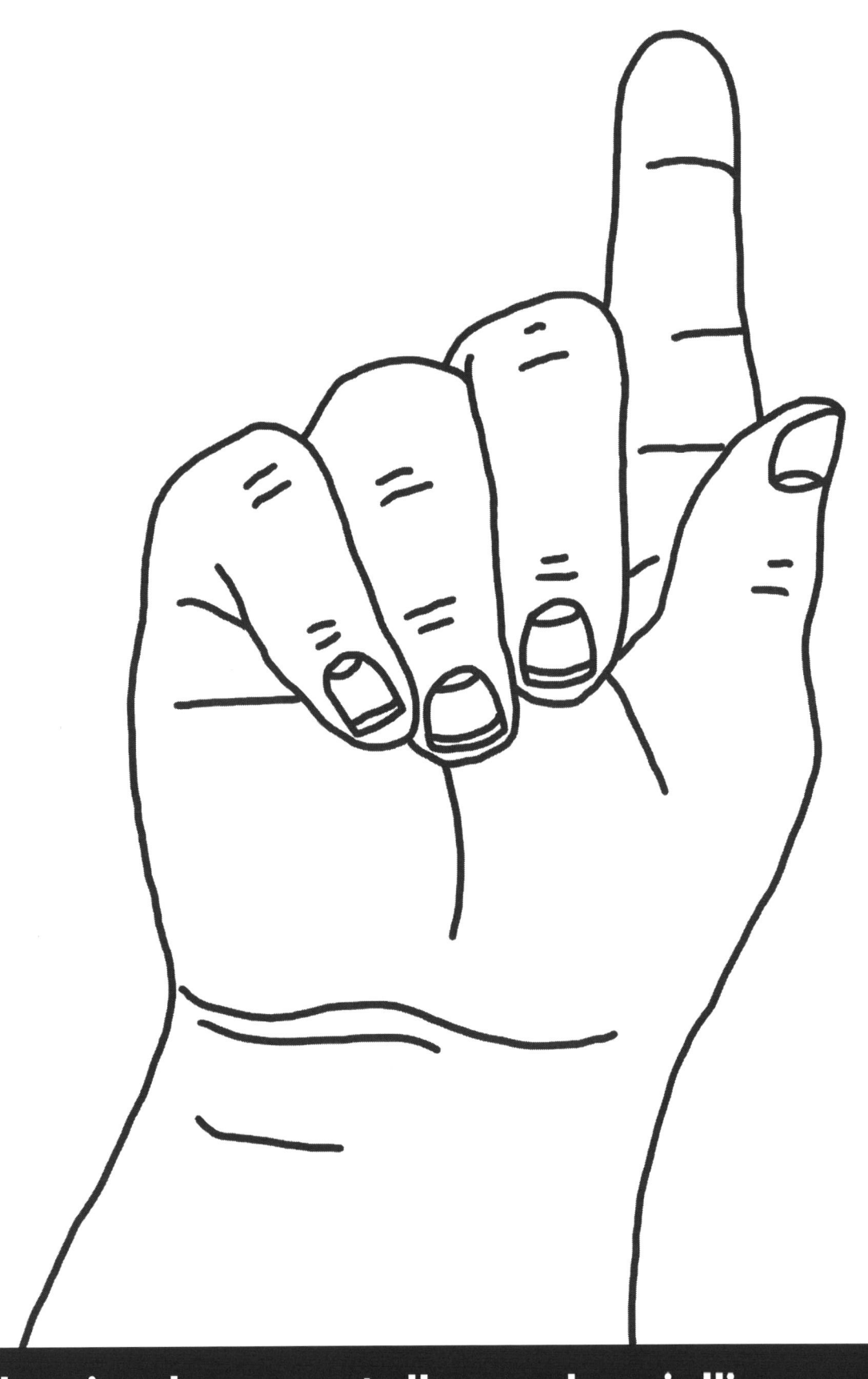

There is only one way to Heaven...Jesus is His name.

Jesus is the Lamb of God Who takes away the sins of the world.

Scripture References

For God so loved the world, that He gave His only begotten Son, that whosoever believeth in Him should not perish, but have everlasting life.

John 3:16

Jesus said, "I am the way, the truth, and the life: no man cometh unto the Father, but by Me."

John 14:6

...Christ died for our sins...He was buried...He rose again the third day according to the scriptures.

I Corinthians 15:3-4

...You are not redeemed with corruptible things...but with the precious blood of Christ.

I Peter 1:18-19

If we confess our sins, He is faithful and just to forgive us our sins, and to cleanse us from all unrighteousness.

I John 1:9

...if thou shalt confess with thy mouth the Lord Jesus, and shalt believe in thine heart that God hath raised Him from the dead, thou shalt be saved. For with the heart man believeth unto righteousness; and with the mouth confession is made unto salvation.

Romans 10:9-10

For by grace are ye saved through faith; and that not of yourselves: it is the gift of God.

Ephesians 2:8

But as many as received Him, to them gave He power to become the sons of God, even to them that believe on His name.

John 1:12

...Christ may dwell in your hearts through faith...

Ephesians 3:17

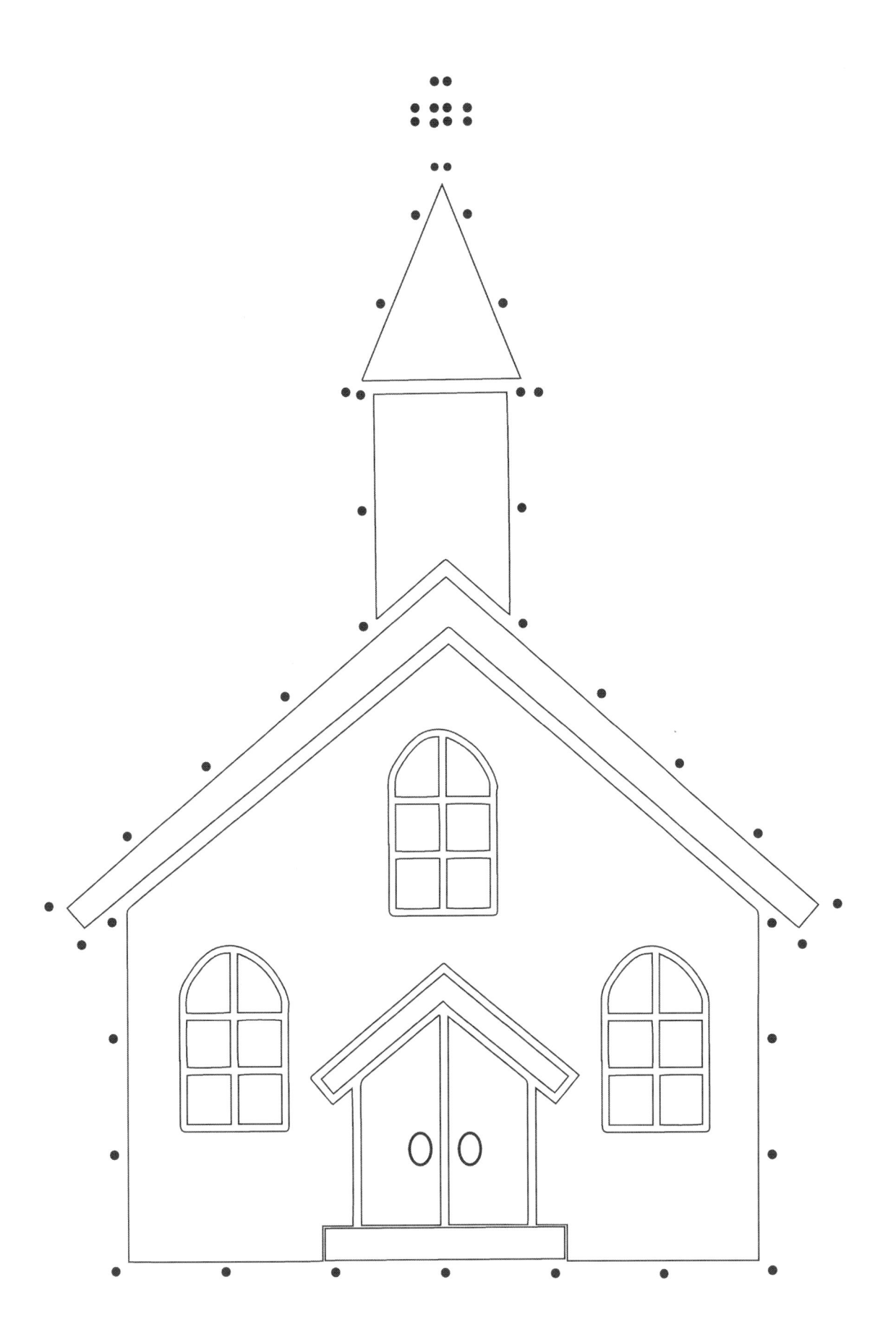

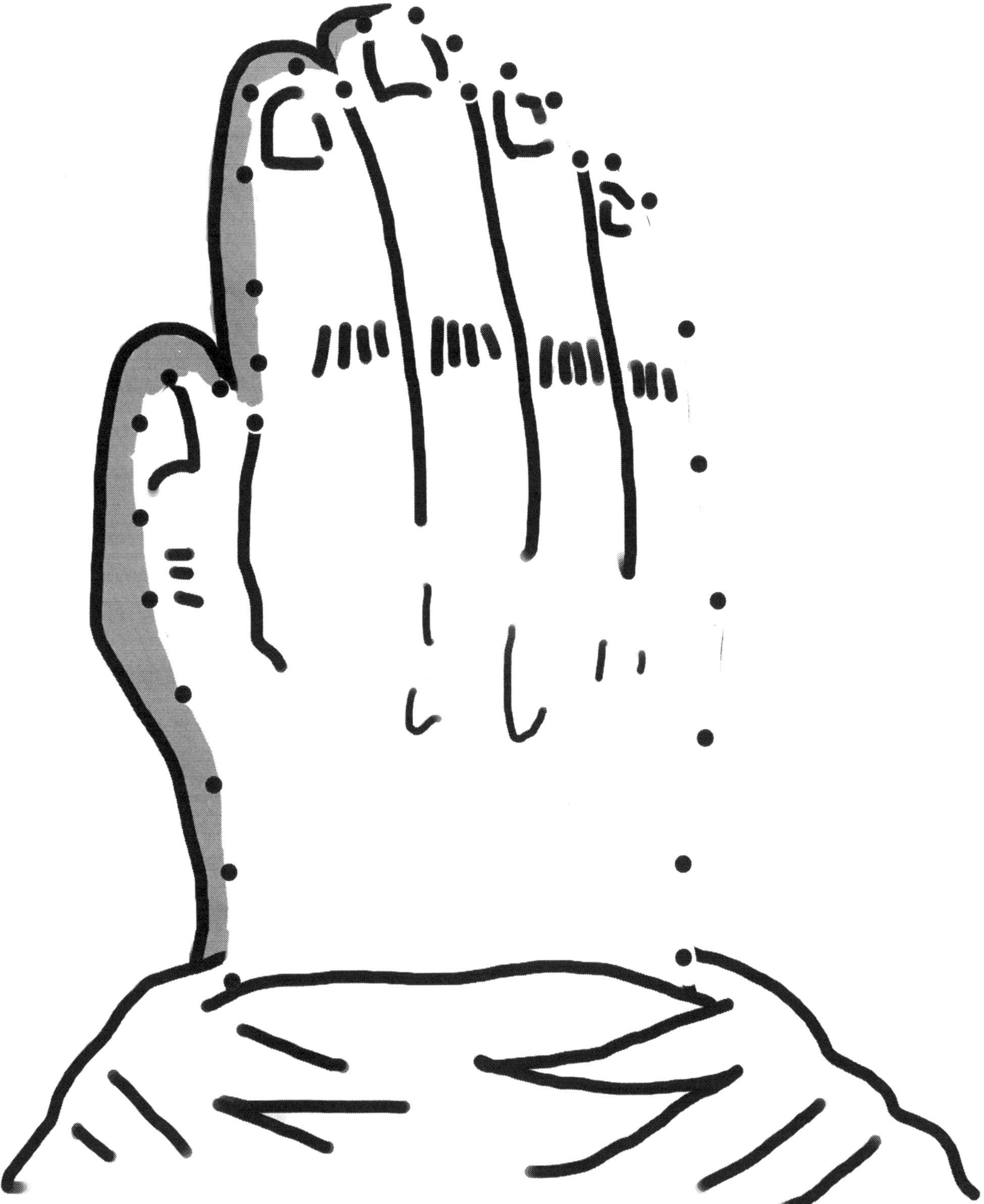

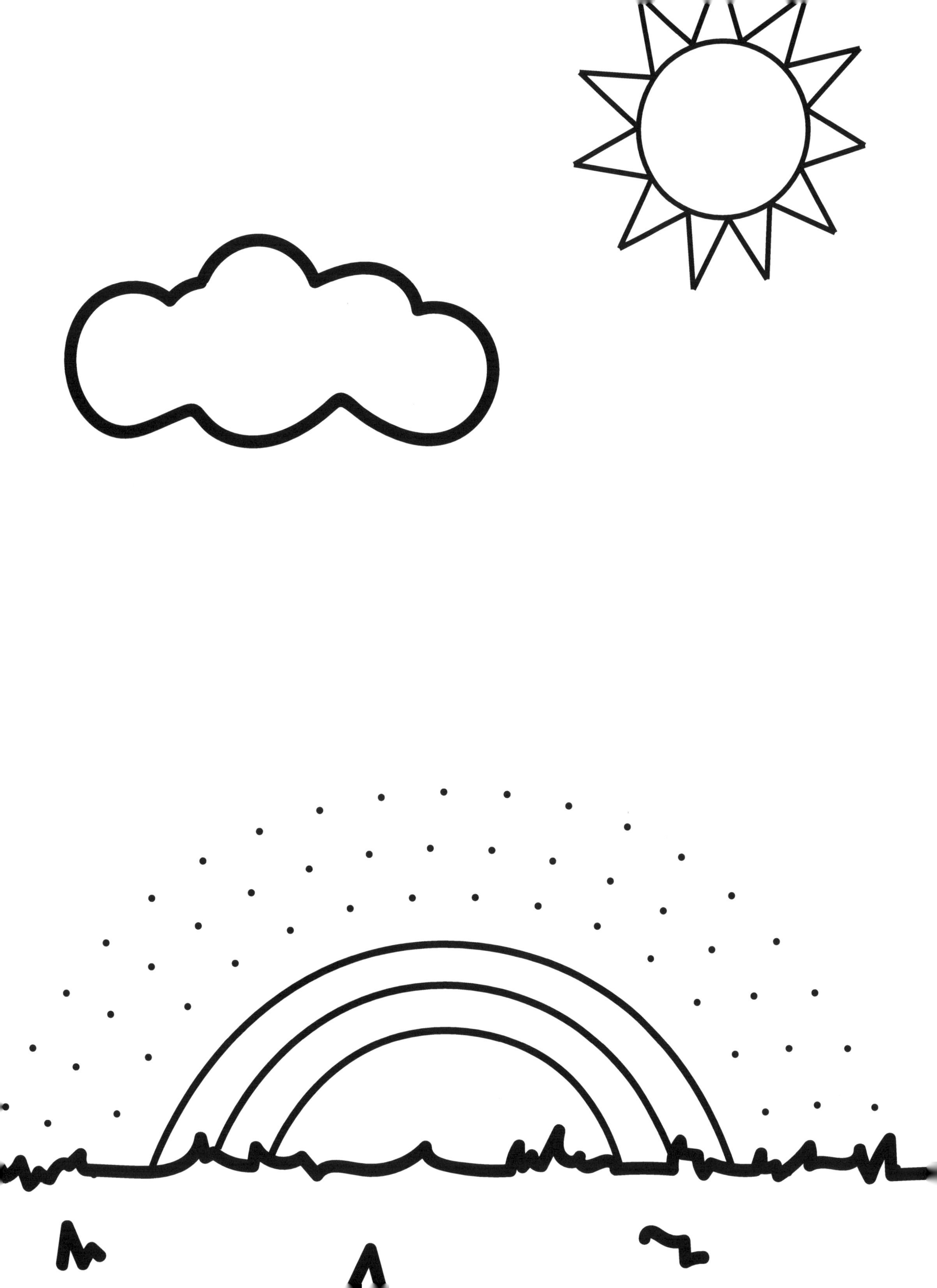

Made in the USA
Columbia, SC
20 January 2025